Peace Be On

Your Home

Presented to:

....

From:

....

Date:

....

Peace
Be On
Your Home

An Illustrated
Treasury

Moody Press
Chicago

Copyright © 1999 Moody Press. Compiled by Jim Bell and Sue Wavre.

Published in the UK by Eagle, an imprint of Inter Publishing Service (IPS) Ltd, PO Box 530, Guildford, Surrey GU2 5FH.

Typeset by Eagle
Printed in Singapore
ISBN No: 0 8024 4626 4

There is no place like home.
  We want it to be a special place, Lord,
    a sanctuary, a haven of peace.
  Of course it isn't always like that.
  Behind the front door lie challenges,
    problems.
  Harmony and forgiveness don't just
    happen;
    they must be cultivated . . .
  Be present in this home, Lord,
    and fill it with Your love.
  May we be mindful of Your loving
    presence.

Joseph T. Sullivan

Almighty God, heavenly Father, You have blessed us with the joy and care of children: Give us calm strength and patient wisdom as we bring them up, that we may teach them to love whatever is just and true and good, following the example of our Savior Jesus Christ. Amen.

The Book of Common Prayer

Contents

Daily Choices

Your home can be a place for dying
or living, for wilting or blooming, for
anxiety or peace, for discouragement
or affirmation, for criticism
or approval, for profane disregard
or reverence, for suspicion or trust,
for blame or forgiveness, for alien-
ation or closeness, for violation or
respect, for carelessness or caring. By
your daily choices, you will make
your home what you want it to be.
Carole Sanderson Streeter

Creating a Home

The best houses seem to 'come from the heart',
and are created by people who know who
they are and express it.
Charlotte Moss

Home is where we belong, it is our space and our place whether for a week, a year or as long as we can foresee. It is where we can just 'be', and also where we can express ourselves in our surroundings, be they a temporary room, a rented apartment or our own house. It is a place of rest from work, but also requires work to keep it going. It is a place of relaxation and of enjoyment in making it interesting, colorful, beautiful and welcoming; where we can thrive rather than passively survive.

Ruth Fowke (adapted)

Style is not what you have, but what you do with what you have.

Emilie Barnes & Yoli Brogger

The only way to provide the right home for your children is to put the Lord above them and fully instruct them in the ways of the Lord. You are responsible before God for the home you provide for them.

Billy Graham

If you are trying to build your home on a good income, success or fame, Satan is going to huff and puff and blow your house down. But if you will build your house on Jesus Christ, on the solid rock of God's Word, Satan can huff and puff while you and your family sit around the fireplace enjoying the blessings of God. This is what God offers to husbands and wives who will build their homes on Him.

Tony Evans

Windows are the smiles of the house.

Emily Post

If you want a golden rule that will fit everybody, this is it: Have nothing in your house that you do not know to be useful, or believe to be beautiful.

William Morris

The actions of creating and maintaining a home become prayer as we deliberately invite Christ to make it his home too.

Ruth Fowke

Home

Peace be to you, and peace be to your house,
and peace be to all that you have.
Book of Samuel

A house is made of walls and beams; a
home is made of love and dreams.

We need not power or splendor,
Wide hall or lordly dome;
The good, the true, the tender,
These form the wealth of home.

Sarah J. Hale

Home may be near,
Home may be far –
But it is anywhere love
And a few plain household treasures are.

Grace Noll Crowell

To know after absence the familiar street and road and village and house is to know again the satisfaction of home.

Hal Borland

The happiness of the domestic fireside is the first boon of heaven; and it is well it is so, since it is that which is the lot of the mass of mankind.

Thomas Jefferson

His house was perfect, whether you liked food, or sleep, or work, or story-telling, or singing, or just sitting and thinking best, or a pleasant mixture of them all.

J.R.R. Tolkien

A comfortable house is a great source of happiness. It ranks immediately after health and a good conscience.

Sydney Smith

Beauty should be important as an inspiration to doing the best with what is at hand for the Christian home-maker.

Edith Schaeffer

Peace unto this house, I pray,
Keep terror and despair away;
Shield it from evil and let sin
Never find lodging room within.
May never in these walls be heard
The hateful or accusing word.
Grant that its warm and mellow light
May be to all a beacon bright . . .

Edgar A. Guest

I have always thought that there is no more fruitful source of discontent than a houeswife's badly cooked dinners and untidy ways. There are now so many good places to eat outside the home, that to compete with them a mistress must be thoroughly acquainted with the theory and practice of cookery, as well as be perfectly conversant with all the other arts of making and keeping a comfortable home.

Isabella Beeton

Ah, what is more blessed than to put cares away, when the mind lays by its burden, and tired of labor with far travel we have come to our own home and rest on the couch we have longed for? This it is which alone is worth all these toils.

Catullus

Home is the resort
Of love, of joy, of peace
and plenty, where,
Supporting and supported,
polish'd friends
And dear relations
mingle into bliss.

Thomson

A good laugh is sunshine in a house.

To put the home on one side and a career on the other as two opposite things —one mundane and only a matter of washing floors, dishes, and ironing clothes, the other fascinating and fulfilling—is to be just plain bankrupt in the area of knowing what life is all about . . .

Edith Schaeffer

Love makes a house a home.

Even though nowadays we have instant food, instant heating, and the seasons make little difference to our homemaking, try to build in happy memories such as these evoked by Laura Ingalls Wilder:

'The little house was fairly bursting with good food stored away for the long winter . . . The fire in the cookstove never went out. At night Pa banked it with ashes to keep the coals alive till morning.

The attic was a lovely place to play. The large, round, colored pumpkins made beautiful chairs and tables. The red peppers and the onions dangled overhead . . . Often the wind howled outside with a cold and lonesome sound. But in the attic Laura and Mary played house with the squashes and the pumpkins, and everything was snug and cosy.'

Laura Ingalls Wilder

Making a home, or creating a healthy environment for a marriage to thrive, begins from within the person. It is primarily spiritual in nature. It's building a relationship where life can grow, where there's nurture for that seed of life that's God-given—a safe place where the soul and spirit can flourish. This is the process that makes home a place of sanctuary, where we can replenish and restore our souls.

Steve and Valerie Bell

What's the good of a home if you are never in it?

George and Weedon Grossmith

A family is a place where principles are hammered and honed on the anvil of everyday living.

Charles Swindoll

Family at Home

*It is in the home that the child learns
the basic principle of accountability
for actions: first to those around him,
and ultimately to God.*
Maxine Hancock

One day when your children are grown and gone, you'll have time for a perfect house. What matters now is not the house, but the home; and not the children's duties, but the children.

Linda Davis Zumbehl

If the most important thing a man can do for his children is to love their mother sacrificially, then the most important thing a mother can do for her children is to respect their father.

Alistair Begg

A clean and orderly house is a joy to everyone, yet there is a need to be sensitive to the greater importance of freedom to paint, mix clay, scatter pieces of cloth in cutting out a dress . . . The possibility of getting soil on a waxed floor is suddenly far less important than the wonder of a tiny box with an exciting mist of green showing that the plants are coming up . . . An atmosphere conducive to creativity must be one of respect for the young (or old) artist—however talented or clumsy the attempt has been—respect for the need for making a mess!

Edith Schaeffer

There is a right time for everything . . . a time to laugh . . .

Ecclesiastes 3:1,4

I'm going to stop punishing my children by saying, 'Never mind! I'll do it myself.'

Erma Bombeck

Some husbands and wives think they are spending time together when, in reality, they are only living in close proximity. They are in the same house at the same time but they are not together. What happens on the emotional level is what counts. Our spending time together in a common pursuit communicates that we care about each other, that we enjoy being with each other, that we like to do things together.

Gary Chapman

The best illustration of the Trinity is the family: a woman and a man who are one, and children who bear the same essence as mom and dad . . . When God created us in his likeness, the first thing he did was make a family.

Tony Evans

And above all these put on love, which binds everything together in perfect harmony.

Colossians 3:14 RSV

We flatter those we hardly know,
We please the fleeting guest,
And deal full many a thoughtless blow
To those who love us best.

Ella Wheeler Wilcox

When I went off to college and came back home, there were certain household rules. If I ate or slept there, then there would be certain things that I needed to do even as an adult visiting there. My father would jokingly remind me, 'This is still my house.' Good humor or not, there is an inescapable sense of responsibility when you live in community with others.

Crawford W. Loritts. Jr.

At work, you think of the children you have left at home. At home, you think of the work you've left unfinished. Such a struggle is unleashed within yourself. Your heart is rent.

Golda Meir

Having family responsibilities and concerns just has to make you a more understanding person.

Sandra Day O'Connor

Communication is the art of expressing in godly ways what is in my heart and of hearing completely and understanding what another feels and thinks. Home is the place for developing these skills.

Ted Tripp

Cleaning your house while your kids are still growing is like shovelling the walk before it stops snowing.

Phyllis Diller

After much experimentation, Len and I have settled on the evening meal as the ideal time and place for growing as a family. Mornings are too pressured, evenings too filled with school work, meetings, phone calls . . .

Catherine Marshall

Mother and Homemaker

The career of motherhood and homemaking is beyond value and needs no justification. Its importance is incalculable.
Katharine Short

Spread love everywhere you go: first of all in your own house.

Give love to your children, to your wife or husband, to a next door neighbor.

Let no one ever come to you without leaving better and happier.

Be the living expression of God's kindness; kindness in your face, kindness in your eyes, kindness in your smile, kindness in your warm greeting.

Mother Teresa

Home-making and child-rearing does not come naturally to many women, but we can all learn. Our attitude and personal security has a lot to do with how we cope.

David Riddell

Did Jesus perceive the thoughts of those in the audience who were thinking, 'I would never go home. Not after my life.' Did he see a housewife look at the ground and a businessman shake his head as if to say, 'I can't start over. I've made too big a mess'? And did he open his arms even wider as if to say, 'Yes. Yes, you can. You can come home'?

Max Lucado

Let the wife make the husband glad to come home, and let him make her sorry to see him leave.

If you are convinced that home-making is worthwhile, then you won't need to apologise. If you can't be confident in saying what you do, then you may need to re-evaluate what you are doing and why.

David Riddell

Learn to say no. Have the courage to stand up to your family and not do everything for them. Moms are often suckers for cleaning up after everyone.

Dr Kevin Leman

A happy homemaker, convinced of her importance as an individual and a contributor to the lives of those around her, forms the backbone of the family. And in turn, good families constitute the building blocks of society. Women in the home, therefore, can exert a crucial influence on their society.

Baukje Doornebal

She gets up before dawn to prepare breakfast for her household, and plans the day's work . . . She watches carefully all that goes on throughout her household, and is never lazy. Her children stand and bless her; so does her husband . . . Charm can be deceptive and beauty doesn't last, but a woman who fears and reverences God shall be greatly praised.

Proverbs 31:15,27,30 LB

A man's home is his wife's castle.

Alexander Chase

Home should be a place of mutual responsibility and respect, of encouragement and cooperation and counsel, of integrity, of willingness to work, of discipline when necessary, with the tempering quality of love added to it, with a sense of belonging, and with someone to talk to.

Richard L. Evans

You are a king by your own fireside, as much as any monarch on his throne.

Cervantes

Don't feel guilty about working if it is important that you do, and don't let the world make you feel uncomfortable at 'staying at home'. Simply make sure you are loving your family, caring for them, showing them how important they are to you, spending time with them, being as creative as possible with the time you have, and ask God to make you the wife, mother, homemaker He wants you to be. However important money is, little is more important than looking after your children.

Sue Wavre

The best way for you and your spouse to guarantee some time without the kids is to do the dishes together.

A mother is a person who seeing there are only four pieces of pie for five people, promptly announces she never did care for pie.

Tenneva Jordan

[The homemaker] strives to make her home a place of beauty, order and security — a positive retreat from a negative and turbulent world . . . realizing that she has the important role of mood-setter and atmosphere-maker for her home.

Linda Davis Zumbehl

Mothers hold their children's hands awhile and their hearts forever.

Anonymous

Mealtimes

Come Lord Jesus be our guest,
And may our meal by you be blest.
attributed to Martin Luther

The preparation and eating of meals is often the core, the pivotal activity, the very heart of a home, especially when they are taken with others . . . Cooking itself is a great opportunity for creative expression, for paying attention to combinations of color, texture, taste and seasonings in the venue, presentation and serving of the meal.

Ruth Fowke

Don't eat watching the TV. Use this mealtime to talk, to laugh, to share what's going on, to teach, to learn, to grow as a family, to get to know others.

Sue Wavre

Every mealtime is a time of giving and receiving, serving and being served . . . Remember someone has worked to pay for the food. Someone has shopped for the food. Someone has prepared it. Someone has cleaned up the dining area and set the table attractively. As the meal begins, someone will pass a dish to you, and you will pass it on to someone else. Everyone is serving and being served.

Paul A. Mickey

Better a meal of vegetables where there is love than a fattened calf with hatred.

Proverbs 15:17

Take my life, and let it be
Consecrated, Lord, to Thee.

Take my moments and my days,
Let them flow in ceaseless praise.

Take my hands and let them move
At the impulse of Thy love.

Take my feet and let them be
Swift and beautiful for Thee.

Take my voice, and let me sing
Always, only, for my King.

Take my lips and let them be
Filled with messages from Thee.

Take my silver and my gold;
Not a mite would I withold.

Take my will, and make it Thine;
It shall be no longer mine.

Frances Ridley Havergal

God in the Home

Unless the LORD builds the house,
its builders labor in vain.
Psalm 127:1

Fix these words of mine in your hearts and minds . . . Teach them to your children, talking about them when you sit at home and when you walk along the road, when you lie down and when you get up.

Deuteronomy 11:18,19

But as for me and my house, we will serve the LORD.

Joshua 24:15 RSV

But seek first the kingdom of God and His righteousness and all these things shall be added to you.

Matthew 6:33 NKJ

The time of business does not with me differ from the time of prayer; and in the noise and clatter of my kitchen, while several persons are at the same time calling for different things, I possess God in . . . . great tranquillity.

Brother Lawrence

What is a home without a Bible? It's a home where daily bread for the body is provided, but the soul is never fed.

I pray that I will allow [God] to rule the raging waves of busyness, that I will be sensitive to His gentle rebukes and His teaching of what is truly important and of eternal value, and allow Him to flood my hectic life with His peace, His calm, His stillness.

What a triumph to go to bed at night with the assurance and satisfaction that I have done all that my heavenly Father wanted me to do. '. . . for so he giveth his beloved sleep' (Psalm 127:2).

Gigi Tchividjian

Hospitality

Share with God's people who are in need.
Practice hospitality.
Romans 12:13

Cheerfully share your home with those who need a meal or a place to stay for the night.

1 Peter 4:9 LB

Blest be that spot, where cheerful
    guests retire
To pause from toil, and trim their ev'n-
    ing fire;
Blest that abode, where want and pain
    repair;
And every stranger finds a ready chair.
Oliver Goldsmith

Prayer of a Teapot

God, You created me
and I am glad;
glad too that I can warm people's hearts
and create home and fellowship.
I am old now and ugly and battered;
made of dull pottery
with a broken stained spout
and a cracked lid.
But I have some pride in myself.
I've a good handle
round which fingers curl snugly and
    confidently.
I pour well too.

Much of the day I sit on the dresser
with bigger and smaller teapots
all in better shape than I.
I really only come to life when I'm used . . .
I feel, God, that You created me to be
    used.
I feel needed and valued
and at the heart of community,
of people who are relaxing,
laughing and talking round the kitchen
    table;
or of people who are in pain and anguish,
Suffering from the shock of bad news.
Use me again and again
that I may know I am alive.

J. de Rooy S.J.

Do not forget to entertain strangers, for by so doing some people have entertained angels without knowing it.

Hebrews 13:2

The art of being a good guest is knowing when to leave.

In the end what really matters is the sharing . . . don't forget that the most wonderful adornment to your home is your spirit of hospitality, your willingness to share your home and your lives with others. Your home will always be its most beautiful when you stretch out your arms in welcome . . .

Emilie Barnes & Yoli Brogger

When God's children are in need, you be the one to help them out. And get into the habit of inviting guests home for dinner or, if they need lodging, for the night.

Romans 12:13 LB

Welcome Home

I thought our home should be properly furnished before others could feel at home.

You said 'Come any time' and when they did, sat them on the floor without a qualm. And the house was properly furnished—with people, with love and with laughter.

I thought that everyday food was for family only; that meals I could offer to guests must have hours of planning and preparation.

You said, 'It will be pot-luck, but you're welcome to share what we have.'

I thought overnight guests were rare creatures, whose coming was a special event.

You said, 'We have an empty bed; stay as long as you need to.'

I thought that our home was our castle.

You said, 'Let down the drawbridge. Having a home is a miracle to be shared.'

Marion Stroud

Work in the Home

Duty makes us do things well,
but love makes us do them beautifully.
Phillip Brooks

Nothing is particularly hard if you divide it into small jobs.

Henry Ford

He who every morning plans the transaction of the day and follows out that plan carries a thread that will guide him through the labyrinth of the most busy life . . . But where no plan is laid . . . chaos will soon reign.

Victor Hugo

A time to keep and a time to throw away.

Ecclesiastes 3:6

Order

I will trust the Lord to bring order into my life and into my house.

In His presence there can be no real chaos and confusion and dirt for He is peace and purity and order—and He is here.

He lives within these walls as He lives within my heart.

He sometimes stops me as I fret and struggle and scold, and says, 'Don't be discouraged.' He reminds me that we are all His untidy children, but He loves us all—even as I love these who cause me so much work.

As I move from room to room picking up other people's possessions, He reminds me how abundant is life that it strews in my family's path so many good things . . . The very earth is strewn with the bright ownings and discards of its living things: sticks and branches and leaves, shells, nests and weeds, and feathers and flowers . . .

He reminds me that behind everything, governing all, is order. Absolute order.

I will trust the Lord to bring that order into my home.

Marjorie Holmes

Prayers for the Homemaker

*Father, I pray that out of your glorious
riches you may strengthen me with power
through your Spirit in my inner being,
so that Christ may dwell in my heart
through faith. That he may make his home,
his permanent home, in my heart.*
from Ephesians 3:16,17

Father, thank you for this place You
have given me to live. I accept it and I
give it back to You to do with as You
please. Release Your flow of creativity in
me through my home as I use it as a tool
of ministry to serve You, my family and
all You send my way.

Quin Sherrer and Laura Watson

Dear Father, make our homes places where You are known, where your Spirit is the air we breathe. May we find in You true joy and peace, through Jesus Christ our Lord.

Katharine Short

Lord, as a wife, may I be of more worth than rubies to my husband, bringing him good and not harm all the days of our lives. Amen

Quin Sherrer (adapted)

Lord of Love, help me welcome those who come to my door today as I would welcome You. Teach me to be a joyful servant.

Sarah Hornsby

Father, please give me wisdom to know how to pray for my family. I lift their specific needs to You now: (*name them*). Please help me to love them with Your love and walk in constant forgiveness.

Lord show me appropriate Scriptures to pray for them. I release _____ into Your hands, and ask You to work in their lives according to Your plan and purpose. I commit them into Your care and trust You to draw them to Yourself by the power of the Holy Spirit. Thank You in Jesus' name for Your work of grace in their lives.

Quin Sherrer (adapted)

Thank you, Lord, for showing me that I tend to make a tight little island of myself, my family and friends. Help me to spread my love to those in need, to those who do not ordinarily attract me.

Catherine Marshall & Leonard Le Sourd

O God my Father, I am ashamed when I remember how so often I hurt most of all those whom I ought to cherish most of all, and how I treat my nearest and dearest in a way in which I would never dare to behave towards strangers. I pray it will not be so today.

Take from me the carelessness, the selfishness, the untidiness . . .

The lack of sensitiveness, which makes me hurt the feelings of others, and never even realise I am doing so.

Take from me the habit of unkind criticism and of nagging fault-finding, the temper of crossness and irritability, which wreck the peace of any home.

Take from me the disobedience, which brings anxiety, and the disloyalty which brings sorrow to those who love me.

Amen.

William Barclay (adapted)

O God, help me always to remember that You have given to me the most important task in the world, the task of making a home.

Help me to remember this when I am tired of making beds, and washing clothes, and cooking meals, and cleaning floors, and mending clothes, and standing in shops. Help me to remember it when I am physically tired in body, and when I am weary in mind with the same things which have to be done again and again, day in and day out.

Help me never to be irritable, never to be impatient, never to be cross. Keep me always sweet. Help me to remember how much my husband and my children need me, and help me not to get annoyed when they take me for granted, and when they never seem to think of the extra work they sometimes cause me.

Help me to make this home such that the family will always be eager to come back to it, and such that, when the children grow up and go out to their own homes, they will have nothing but happy memories of the home from which they have come.

This I ask for Your love's sake. Amen

William Barclay

There is no place like home.
  We want it to be a special place, Lord,
    a sanctuary, a haven of peace.
  Of course it isn't always like that.
  Behind the front door lie challenges,
    problems.
  Harmony and forgiveness don't just
    happen;
    they must be cultivated . . .
  Be present in this home, Lord,
    and fill it with Your love.
  May we be mindful of Your loving
    presence.

Joseph T. Sullivan

Almighty God, heavenly Father, You have blessed us with the joy and care of children: Give us calm strength and patient wisdom as we bring them up, that we may teach them to love whatever is just and true and good, following the example of our Savior Jesus Christ. Amen.

The Book of Common Prayer

Lord, the next time I find myself thinking, 'I'm only playing with the children,' or 'I'm only sorting the washing,' help me to stop saying 'only'. Even when I'm tired, help me to surrender my activity to You, so that I can give myself fully to what needs doing. Let me remember that this is Your will for me, here and now, and show me how to receive the good things and the gladness that You offer me.

Angela Ashwin

Text Credits

Care has been taken to attribute all quotes from all sources, and to clear all permissions. We are grateful to the following for their permission and apologise for any unintentional omissions. The full works of the Moody Press authors quoted is also listed.

Ashwin, Angela, p 82, *Patterns not Padlocks* (Guildford: Eagle Publishing, 1992).

Barclay, William, p 76, *The Plain Man's Book of Prayers* (London: Fontana); p 78, *More Prayers for the Plain Man* (London: Fontana, 1962).

Barnes, Emilie & Brogger, Yoli, pp 12, 63, *Beautiful Home on a Budget* (Eugene, Oregon: Harvest House Publishers, 1998).

Beeton, Isabella, p 21: Preface to first edition of *Mrs Beeton's Book of Household Management*.

Begg, Alistair, p 28; works published by Moody Press: *What Angels Wish They Knew: The Basics of True Christianity*, 1999; *Lasting Love: How to Avoid Marital Failure*, 1997; *Made for His Pleasure: Ten Benchmarks of a Vital Faith*, 1996.

Bell, Steve and Valerie, p 26, *Made to be Loved: Enjoying Spiritual Intimacy with God and Your Spouse* (Chicago, Moody Press,1999).

Brooks, Phillip, p 66: quoted in *Beautiful Home on a Budget*, op. cit.

Chapman, Gary, p 32, *The Five Love Languages*. Works published by Moody Press: *The Other Side of Love: Handling Anger In A Godly Way*, 1999; *Parenting Your Adult Child: How You Can Help Them Achieve Their Full Potential*, 1999; *Loving Solutions: Overcoming Barriers in Your Marriage*, 1998; *Five Signs of a Loving Family*, 1998; *The Five Love Languages of Children*, 1997; *Toward a Growing Marriage: Building the Love Relationship of Your Dreams*, 1996; *Hope for the Separated: Wounded Marriages Can Be Healed*, 1996; *The Five Love Languages: How to Express Heartfelt Commitment to Your Mate*, 1992.

Crowell, Grace Noll, p 16; seen in *Blessings of Home* (Eugene, Oregon: Harvest House Publishers, 1998).

de Rooy, J., S.J., p 61, *Tools for Meditation* (Pinner, Middlesex: Grail Publications, UK).

Doornebal, Baukje, p 40: *Homemaking* (Colorado Springs: NavPress, 1981).

Evans, Tony, p 12: *Are Christians Destroying America?*; p 32: *Our God Is Awesome*. Other works published by Moody Press: *Who Is This King of Glory?: Experiencing The Fullness of Christ's Work in Our Lives*, 1999; *The Battle Is the Lord's: Waging Victorious Spiritual Warfare*, 1998; *What Matters Most: Four Absolute Necessities in Following Christ*, 1997; *Returning to Your First Love: Putting God Back in First Place*, 1995; *The Promise: Experiencing God's Greatest Gift*, 1996; *Our God is Awesome: Encountering the Greatness of Our God*, 1994; *Are Christians Destroying*

America?: How to Restore a Decaying Culture, 1996; *Tony Evans Speaks Out On Divorce and Remarriage*, 1995; *Tony Evans Speaks Out On Gambling and the Lottery*, 1995; *Tony Evans Speaks Out On Sexual Purity*, 1995; *Tony Evans Speaks Out On Single Parenting*, 1995.

Fowke, Ruth, pp 11, 15, 49, *Creativity and Prayer* (Guildford: Eagle Publishing, 1998).

Guest, Edgar A., p 20, seen in *Blessings of Home*, op. cit.

Hancock, Maxine, p 28, *Creative, Confident Children*, seen in *Women's Wisdom Through the Ages* (Wheaton, Illinois: Harold Shaw Publishers, 1994).

Holmes, Marjorie, p 68: *I've Got to Talk to Somebody, God* (London: Hodder & Stoughton, 1969).

Hornsby, Sarah, p 72: *Love Is . . .* (Grand Rapids: Chosen Books, 1993).

Leman, Dr Kevin, p 40: *Bonkers* (Grand Rapids, MI: Baker Book House, 1987)

Loritts, Crawford W. Jnr., p 35: *Never Walk Away: Lessons on Integrity from a Father Who Lived It* (Chicago, Moody Press, 1998); *A Passionate Commitment: Recapturing Your Sense of Purpose*, 1996.

Lucado, Max, p 38: *Six Hours One Friday*, (Nashville, TN, Word Publishing, 1995)

Marshall, Catherine, p 36, *A Closer Walk* (London: Hodder & Stoughton, 1987); p 74, Catherine Marshall & Leonard Le Sourd, *My Personal Prayer Diary* (London: Hodder & Stoughton, 1988).

Mickey, Paul A. with Proctor, William, p 50: *Tough Marriage* (William Morrow & Co, 1986).

Mother Teresa, p 37, seen in *Blessings of Home*, op. cit.

Post, Emily, p 15, quoted in *Beautiful Home on a Budget*, op. cit.

Riddell, David, pp 38, 40, *Living Wisdom* (Guildford: Eagle Publishing, 1996).

Schaeffer, Edith, pp 20, 22, 31. *What Is a Family?* (London: Hodder & Stoughton, 1976).

Sherrer, Quin and Watson, Laura, p 71: *A House of Many Blessings* (Guildford: Eagle Publishing, 1993); pp 72, 74, Quin Sherrer with Ruthanne Garlock, *How to Pray for Your Family and Friends* (Eastbourne: Kingsway, 1991).

Short, Katharine, pp 37, 72: *Reflections* (Oxford: Lion Publishing, 1981).

Streeter, Carole Sanderson, p 8: *Finding Your Place After Divorce*, seen in *Women's Wisdom Through the Ages* (Wheaton, Illinois: Harold Shaw Publishers, 1994).

Stroud, Marion, p 65: *The Gift of Marriage* (Oxford: Lion Publishing, 1982).

Sullivan, Joseph T., p 81: *Good Night, Lord* (out of print). With kind permission of the author.

Swindoll, Charles, p 26: *Devotions for Growing Strong in the Seasons of Life* (Nashville, TN, Word Publishing, 1994).

Tchividjian, Gigi, p 56: *A Woman's Search for Serenity* (Fleming H. Revell Co., 1981).

Thomson, p 22: seen in *Blessings of Home*, D. Morgan (Eugene, Oregon: Harvest House Publishers, 1998).

TimTiley Prints prayer card, p 51, © TFTT.

Tripp, Ted, p 36: *Shepherding a Child's Heart*, 1996.

Unmarked quotes, pp 16, 22, 38, 45, 54, 63: *God's Little Devotional Books*. Published by Eagle Publishing. Copyright Honor Books, Tulsa, Oklahoma.

Wilder, Laura Ingalls, p 25, *Little House in the Big Woods* (London: Random House, 1932).

Zumbehl, Linda Davis, pp 28, 46: *Homebodies* (Springfield, PA: Whitaker House, 1991).

Picture Credits

p 5, *East End Farm, Moss Lane, Pinner* (detail), Helen Allingham, 1848–1926. FAPL/Polak Gallery, London.

p 9, *Waxwell Farm, Pinner*, Helen Allingham, 1848–1926. Eagle Publishing.

p 10, *A Willing Helper* (detail), Michael Munkacsy, 1844–1909. FAPL/Gavin Graham Gallery.

p 13, *The Return of the Gleaners*, Myles Birket Foster, 1825–1899. FAPL/Polak Gallery, London.

p 14, *Un Jour en Eté*, Patrick William Adam, 1854–1929. FAPL/Paisnel Gallery.

p 17, *A Sunday Afternoon*, Carl Christian Frederik Thomsen, 1847–1912. FAPL/Private Collection.

p 19, *A Family Gathering*, Joseph Clark, 1834–1926. FAPL/ Haynes Fine Art.

p 23, *The Chimney Corner*, 1878, Joseph Clark, 1834–1912. Christopher Wood Gallery, London.

p 24, *The Youngest Child*, William Henry Knight, 1823–1863. Sotheby's, Bond St, London.

p 27, *Helping Mother*, George Washington Brownlow, 1835–1876. FAPL/Haynes Fine Art.

p 29, *Time for Tea*, George Goodwin Kilburne, 1839–1924. FAPL/Waterhouse & Dodd.

p 30, *Dividing the Spoils*, Paul Seignac, 1826–1904. Burlington Paintings, London. FAPL.

p 33, *Bubbles*, William Hemsley, 1819–c.1893. Sotheby's, Bond St, London.

p 34, *A Willing Helper* (detail), Michael Munkacsy, see p 10.

p 39, *Golden Hours*, Hans Tichy, 1861–1925. FAPL/Julian Simon Fine Art.

p 41, *The New Baby* (detail), Myles Birket Foster, 1825–1899. FAPL.

p 43, *The Finishing Touch*, Charles Haigh Wood, 1856–1927. FAPL/Haynes Fine Art.

p 44, *Breakfast Time*, 1901, Harry Brooker, 1848–1940. Richard Green Gallery, London.

p 47, *Un Jour en Eté*, Henri-Gaston Darien, 1864–1926. FAPL/Galerie Berko.

p 48, *Making Apple Pie* (detail), Gustave Auguste Hessl, 1849–1926. FAPL/Polak Gallery.

p 53, *A Cottage Well* (detail), Myles Birket Foster, 1825–1899. Anthony Mitchell. FAPL.

p 55, *A Garden in October, Aldworth* (detail), Helen Allingham, 1848–1926. Eagle Publishing.

p 57, *Hollyhocks,* Helen Allingham, 1848–1926. Eagle Publishing.

p 58, *Pine Tree Cottage,* Helen Allingham, 1848–1926. FAPL/Polak Gallery, London.

p 60, *Morning Chapter,* Charles Spencelayh, 1865–1958. Bridgeman Art Library/Christie's Images, London.

p 62, *The Peaceful Village,* Henry John Yeend King, 1855–1924. FAPL/Cambridge Fine Art.

p 64, *Christmas Cheer,* George Sheridan Knowles, 1863–1931. FAPL/ Private Collection.

p 67, *Washing Day,* 1878, Pierre Edouard Frere, 1819–1886. FAPL.

p 69, *Bluebell Wood, Kent,* Helen Allingham, 1848–1926. Eagle Publishing.

p 70, *Mrs Chandler in her Room,* Robert Jenkins Onderdonk, 1853–1917. Anthony Mitchell.

p 73, *The Labourer's Welcome,* Joseph Clark, 1834–1912. Sheffield Art Galleries.

p 75, *A Summer Idyll,* Henry John Yeend King, 1855–1924. FAPL/ Sutcliffe Galleries.

p 77, *Domestic Instructions* (detail), Isidore Patrois, 1915–1884. FAPL/ Gavin Graham Gallery.

p 79, *Golden Hours* (detail), Hans Tichy; see p 39.

p 80, *A Stream by a Cottage Door, Ockley, Surrey,* Arthur Claude Strachan, 1865–1954. FAPL/Galerie George.

p 83, *Helping Mother* (detail), George Washington Brownlow, see p 27.